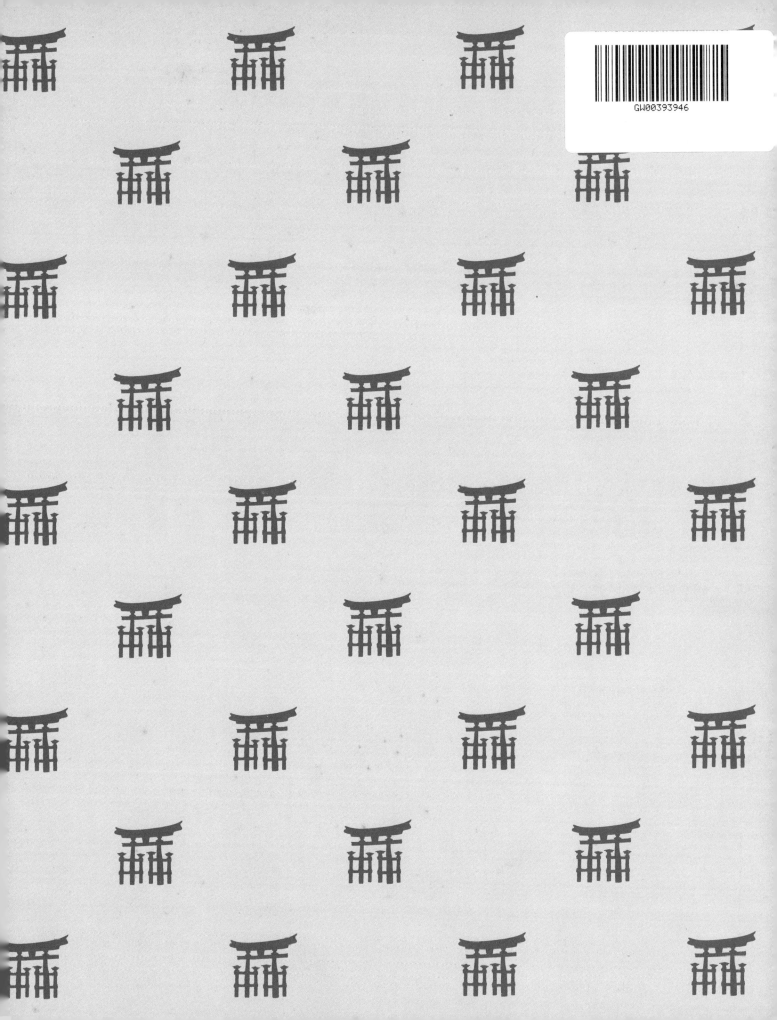

THE
JAPANESE

Clare Doran

Wayland

Look into the Past

The Ancient Chinese
The Anglo-Saxons
The Aztecs
The Egyptians
The Greeks
The Incas
The Japanese
The Maya
The Normans
The Romans
The Sioux
The Tudors & Stuarts
The Victorians
The Vikings

Series editor: Joanna Bentley
Series designer: David West
Book designer: Joyce Chester

First published in 1994 by Wayland (Publishers) Ltd,
61 Western Road, Hove, East Sussex, BN3 1JD, England.

© Copyright 1994 Wayland (Publishers) Ltd

British Library Cataloguing in Publication Data
Doran, Clare
    Japanese.—(Look into the
    Past Series)
    I. Title   II. Series
    952

ISBN 0 7502 1261 6

Typeset by Dorchester Typesetting Group Ltd., Dorset,
England.
Printed and bound in Italy by L.E.G.O. S.p.A., Vicenza,
Italy.

While every effort has been made to trace the copyright
holders of all pictures, in some cases it has proved
impossible. The publishers apologise for this apparent
negligence.

Picture acknowledgements
The publishers would like to thank the following for
supplying the pictures in this book: Ancient Art and
Architecture Collection 8, 15 (both), 17 (top), 23 (bottom),
25 (both), 28; Chapel Studios 29 (top); E. T. Archive 17
(bottom, Victoria & Albert Museum), 27 (bottom right);
Edo-Tokyo Museum 11 (bottom), 14, 20, 24 (left); Robert
Harding 10 (Nigel Blythe), 18 (right), 21 (bottom), 22;
Suzanne Perrin 5 (bottom); Shin'enKan Foundation 21
(top); Tokyo National Museum 11 (top), 13 (top), 16, 27
(top right); Wayland Picture Library 12; Werner Forman
Archive 5 (top, Kuroda Collection), 6, 9 (both, L J
Anderson Collection), 13 (bottom, Kita-In, Saitumi), 18
(left), 26 (Kita-In, Saitumi).
Map artwork on page 4 by Jenny Hughes.

CONTENTS

Words that appear in **bold italic** in the text are explained in the glossary on page 30.

THE BIRTH OF A CITY

Japan is a country that is made up of four main islands and many smaller islands. They lie in the Pacific Ocean, to the east of China. Japan has gone through many changes throughout its history. We are going to look at a famous period, when the city of Edo became Japan's capital in the seventeenth century. This was the time of *samurai* warriors and leaders called *shoguns*.

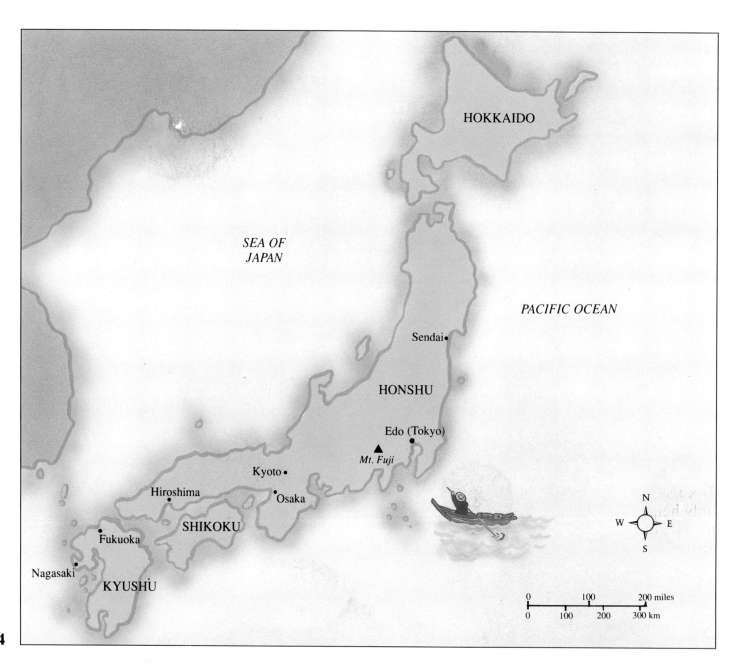

For hundreds of years the different provinces of Japan were fighting each other, and the country was not under one ruler. Peace finally came to Japan in 1603. The man who brought about this peace was called Tokugawa Ieyasu. As a reward, the Emperor of Japan gave Ieyasu the title 'shogun'. This title means 'Commander-in-Chief for beating the barbarians'. The shogun made the village of Edo his home. This village was to grow into one of the largest and most lively cities in the world at that time. Many years later the name of this city would change to Tokyo, the present capital of Japan.

Tokugawa Ieyasu not ▶ only helped to set up the city of Edo, but also started a new period of Japanese history. This stretch of history lasted for 250 years and is called the Edo period.

EDO CITY

Ieyasu brought his loyal lords to Edo but it took many years to change the muddy fishing village into a powerful city. Roads had to be built and marshes filled so that the land could be used. Bridges were built over the many rivers and canals were dug so that food and other materials could be moved easily from place to place. The biggest danger to Edo was fire. Fires would often start after earthquakes. Fires were so common they were called the 'flowers of Edo'. They would often destroy large areas of the city.

Edo Castle become a sign of the power and strength of the shogun. Over a number of years, the castle grew larger and grander. When the castle was finished, it had sixty-six gates and thirty-six guard posts.

▲ Inside the grounds there were bridges, ponds and stables. This picture of Nijo Castle in Kyoto shows us what a Japanese castle looks like. Here you can see a wide moat and decorated roof tiles.

This bridge, called Nihonbashi, was the centre of Edo city and was called the 'bridge of Japan'. The five main roads that spread through Japan started from this bridge. All kinds of people from the very rich to the very poor would pass Nihonbashi.

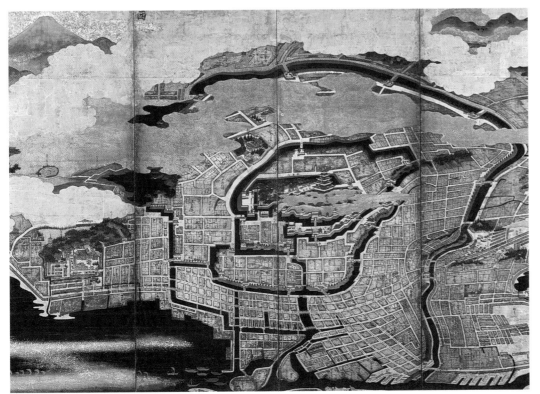

This picture is a plan of Edo city. You can see boats coming in at the bottom left. Waterways were very important for transport throughout Japan.

Temples were built to the north-east of the city. The north-east was thought to be an unlucky direction, so temples were built there to protect the city from bad luck that might come from this direction.

7

THE PEOPLE OF EDO

People were divided into four main groups, depending on their family background and the work they did. These ideas had come originally from China as part of a system of thinking called *Confucianism.* The four main classes in order of importance were the warrior class, also known as the samurai, the farmers, the craftsmen, and the merchants.

The samurai were seen as the top of society and were supposed to set a good example to the ordinary people. Only samurai were allowed to wear two swords. In this painting you can see samurai wearing a long sword and a short sword. Samurai also had a special hairstyle. They would shave the front of their heads and tie the rest of the hair into a ponytail which was doubled over.

The smaller piece of armour shown here was made to give to a boy when he reached the age of fourteen. At this time his hair would also be dressed in an adult style. The samurai armour had a breast plate to protect the chest and pieces to protect the legs, arms and neck. The design of the helmet was important. It might be in the shape of an animal. A samurai believed the helmet would help him look frightening and would scare the enemy. ▼

▲ This close-up shows how bright pieces of cord were placed over the iron of the armour. The sleeves of this armour were based on armour owned by a famous Japanese warrior called Minamoto Yoshitsune.

THE FARMERS

The largest group of people in Edo Japan were the farmers. The farmers were seen as very important because they grew the country's rice. Rice was so precious that some people's wealth was decided not by how much money they had, but by how much rice their land could grow. However, the farmers' lives were very hard. They would work outdoors all day, and even in the evenings they had no time to relax but were busy making sacks and ropes out of straw. There were times when there would be little food to eat, or bad weather would make their job very difficult.

Growing rice took a lot of time and involved every member of the family. The fields were flooded with water for the young rice plants to grow. The members of the family worked together; planting, watering, weeding and harvesting the rice. It is still grown in the same way today.

東海道
五拾三次
之内
蒲原
夜之雪

During the cold weather a farmer wore a cloak made of straw and a hat made of bamboo. His sandals were also made of straw, and pieces of cloth were tied around his legs and lower arms for extra warmth.

The farmers' houses varied a lot from region to region. Often the roofs were made of thatch and were low so that snow would easily fall off them. The family would sit around the fire, which they also used for cooking.

THE CRAFTSMEN

As more people moved from the countryside and came to live in the city of Edo, the job of the craftsmen became more important because many new buildings were needed. Craftsmen learnt their trade by starting out as *apprentices* when they were very young. They left their own families to live with a master who would teach them his skill. If he was lucky, the apprentice would take over the master's business when he grew old. The ordinary people of the town lived in small, narrow houses. They went to a public bath every day. Here, as well as getting clean, they would meet their friends and catch up on the local gossip.

The people in this picture are sword-grinders. Their job was to keep sharp the swords of the samurai. People believed swords had a special power and it was important to look after them carefully. Here we can see the sword-grinders sharpening a sword. What do you think the man is carrying in his box? ▼

◄ There were many different types of craftsmen in Edo. Many were involved with the making of buildings, such as plasterers, carpenters, stonemasons or roofers. The famous artist, Hokusai, drew many craftsmen, capturing the movement of their bodies as they lifted and strained.

▲ Here you can see a young boy selling fresh cold water in the streets. He wears a straw hat to protect his head from the sun.

THE MERCHANTS

According to the government the merchants had the lowest position in Edo society as they did not make useful products such as swords, or rice, but earned their living by selling other people's work. However, during this period of history, the merchants were to play a very important role, setting up shops, helping trade grow and also lending money to the samurai. The government tried to pass laws stopping the merchants from showing off their new wealth. For example, they were not supposed to wear expensive silk clothes. The merchants would break this law by lining the inside of their clothes with brightly coloured silk.

The Mitsui family was a powerful merchant family. By 1700 their shop, called Echigoya, had become Japan's largest store. They brought in the idea of selling goods at a definite price, rather than deciding with each customer what the price should be. They also sold material cut to the size that the customer wanted, rather than one large piece of material.

There were many different types of money in Edo Japan. Gold, silver, copper and iron coins were used. This large gold coin is called an Oban and was used only on very special occasions.

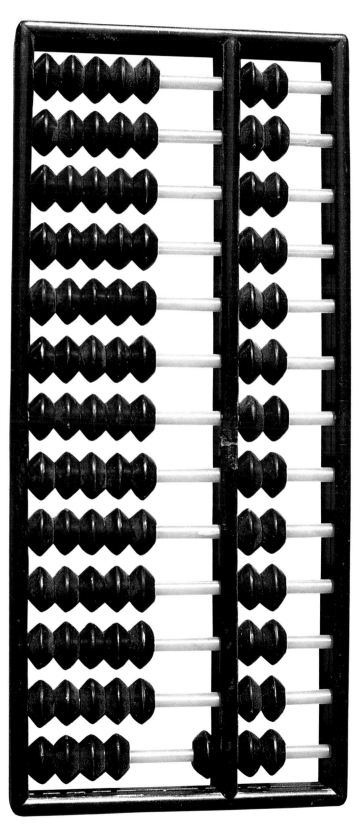

◄ Inside a shop the usual way of working out a bill was by using a piece of equipment made of beads called an **abacus**. Not only would the shopkeeper be able to add up numbers, but he could also subtract, multiply and divide very quickly indeed.

TRANSPORT AND TRAVEL

The Edo period was a time when travel became possible for more people. People would travel for business as well as for pleasure. A number of roads had been built to link the city of Edo with other towns and cities. The most famous road was called the Tokaido. However, people were not allowed to go on a journey whenever they wanted. There were special gates across parts of the road where travellers would be checked to see if they had the right papers from their local government office which allowed them to travel.

◀ As there were more people travelling for business and pleasure, there needed to be more places for them to rest and eat along the way. Travellers could stop, rest and be entertained for the evening at the various *tea-houses* and inns that appeared on roadsides. Sometimes they would spend all their money before they reached the end of their journey.

There are many ▶ mountains in Japan, so transport by road was very difficult. The main way of moving goods was by sea and there were thousands of boats moving between the large city of Osaka and Edo.

◄ Ferry boats were used to help people cross rivers. When there were no boats, people sat on the shoulders of **porters** who carried them across the river.

THE THEATRE

Several types of theatre were popular in Japan at this time. For the samurai, a type of drama called *Noh* drama was popular. This was mostly slow-moving and serious, with a religious feel about it. For the ordinary people *kabuki* was an exciting and popular form of entertainment. The leading kabuki actors were famous throughout the whole country and books were written about them, praising their handsome appearance and acting skills. Another important form of drama was called *Bunraku*. Instead of actors, puppets were used to act the story while singers and musicians provided music and songs.

Colourful make-up and ornate, eye-catching costumes were worn by kabuki actors. The plays were full of action, with the entrances and the exits of the actors on to the stage being particularly exciting. The audience would shout out their comments even during the performance. Going to the kabuki theatre was an important day out, with plays lasting all day and people eating, drinking and enjoying each other's company.

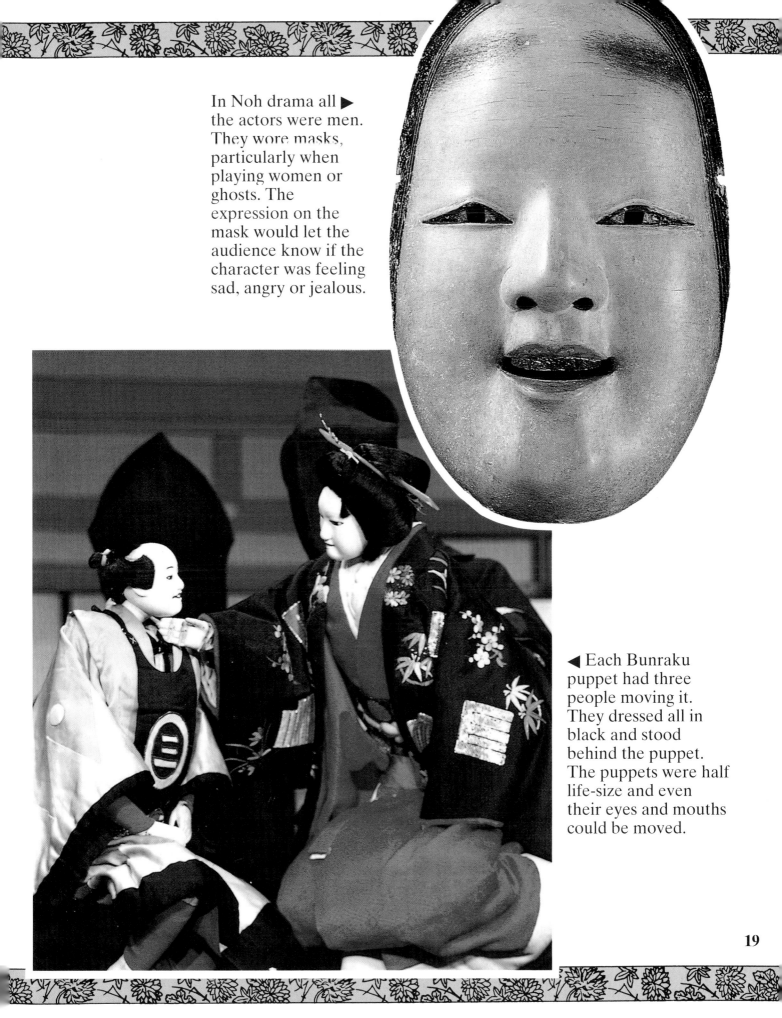

In Noh drama all ▶ the actors were men. They wore masks, particularly when playing women or ghosts. The expression on the mask would let the audience know if the character was feeling sad, angry or jealous.

◀ Each Bunraku puppet had three people moving it. They dressed all in black and stood behind the puppet. The puppets were half life-size and even their eyes and mouths could be moved.

THE PLEASURE QUARTERS

Although the government of Edo wanted people to work as hard as possible, there were also places where people would escape from work and enjoy themselves. One popular place was the Yoshiwara, where mostly men went to eat, drink, gamble and relax. It was a long journey from the centre of Edo, and part of the journey was by boat. Samurai were not supposed to go there, but they would hide their heads under large hats and sneak in. At night the Yoshiwara was completely closed up. If a visitor had not left in time, they would have to stay until the morning. Once inside the Yoshiwara, it was so different to ordinary life that it was called 'the floating world'.

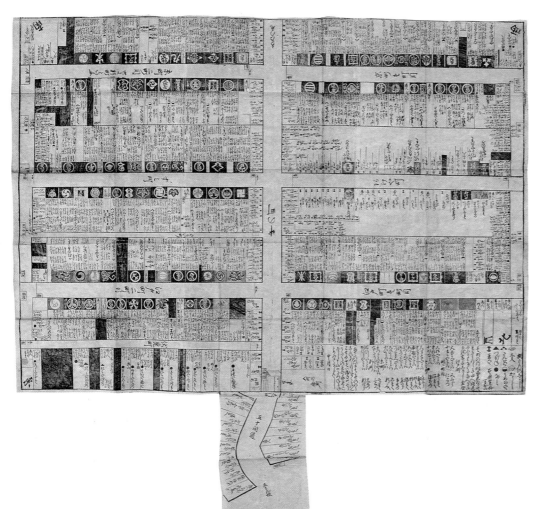

This plan shows the layout of the huge area of Yoshiwara.

As well as having places to eat, drink and gamble, the Yoshiwara was famous for its beautiful women. There were many different types of entertainers, both male and female, but the most important of all were called **geisha.** The geisha were a special group of women who had been taught how to dance, sing and even talk in an elegant fashion from a young age.

The way geisha ▶ looked and dressed was very important. They covered their faces in a white powder and wore heavy wigs. Their shoes were sometimes so high they needed a maid to help them walk! However, life for most of the ordinary women was very hard. Sometimes they were so unhappy they would run away. Usually they were caught and quickly brought back.

RELIGIONS

There were a number of different religions and philosophies that the Japanese people of this time followed. The oldest religion of Japan is called *Shintoism.* Another important religion was Buddhism, which came to Japan in the sixth century AD. Most people followed both religions, visiting both Shinto *shrines* and Buddhist temples.

People worshipped at holy places called shrines, and sometimes even at a rock or a mountain which was believed to be sacred.

In the early ▶
eighteenth century a
large Buddhist temple
called Todaiji was
repaired and rebuilt.
The main statue,
called the Great
Buddha, is sixteen
metres high. This is
still the largest bronze
statue in the world
and the building
where you can see
this statue is the
largest wooden
building in the world.

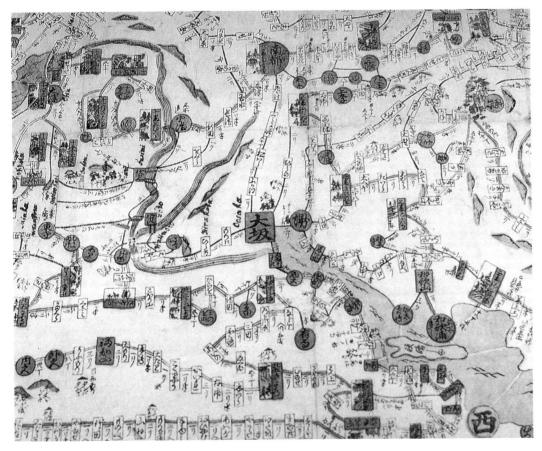

◀ During the Edo
period it became
popular to go on a
pilgrimage, both for
religious reasons and
as a good excuse to
travel. Special maps
were used by pilgrims
to visit holy places.
This map shows thirty
places that a pilgrim
could visit to worship
a god called Kannon.

THE WRITTEN WORD

Most of the ordinary people in the city of Edo could read, so books were very popular. There were many serious books telling people how to lead good lives, or containing facts about law or science. However, people also read books for fun. There were books full of love stories, or stories of great warriors of the past. As well as buying them from bookshops, people could borrow books from a lending library.

◄ Books were printed from wooden printing blocks like this. You can see how the shapes of the letters have been carved into the wood. The books could then be printed very cheaply.

Wooden blocks like this were also used to make art prints. For very little money, you could buy a print of a famous beautiful woman or, as in this picture, of your favourite actor. ▶

ARTS AND CRAFTS

The people at this time were very interested in the latest fashions – especially those living in the large cities of Edo, Osaka and Kyoto. If they could, they would spend large amounts of money buying expensive clothes. As the merchants became richer they also wanted to have beautiful objects in their houses. There were many artists producing beautiful pieces of art and *ceramics*. People were also interested in learning about the arts, and classes in poetry writing, Japanese dance or the *tea ceremony* became popular.

The *kimono* was a long piece of cloth which ▶ was tied around the body with a wide belt. The design of the kimono material was carefully chosen to suit the age of the wearer and even the right time of year.

◀ Here you can see a group of lacquer workers. They carefully prepare wooden boxes, then decorate them beautifully.

▲ Here you can see a famous writing case designed by the artist Ogata Korin (1658-1716). In the design you can see a bridge and flowers made of pearl. People at this time knew that Korin was referring to a story famous in Japanese literature. Korin was famous for his clever designs and bright use of colours, especially on pottery.

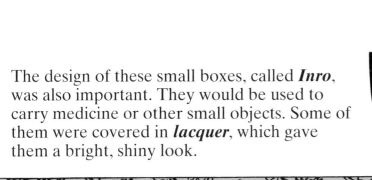

The design of these small boxes, called ***Inro***, was also important. They would be used to carry medicine or other small objects. Some of them were covered in ***lacquer***, which gave them a bright, shiny look.

27

THE SEASONS AND FESTIVALS

During the year there were several festivals. New Year was an important holiday season in Edo Japan. People visited friends, relatives and people they worked with. Special foods, such as small cakes made of rice, were eaten. During the summer there was a festival of the dead, when people, especially in the villages, would sing songs and perform dances. Many of the festivals were linked with nature and the seasons, such as looking at maple leaves in the autumn.

◀ In spring people would enjoy a trip to see the cherry blossoms. Some places were famous for particularly beautiful cherry blossoms. At these places, there would be large crowds of people sitting under the trees, eating, drinking and looking at the blossoms.

The boys' festival was celebrated on 5 May. A kite in the shape of a carp fish was flown outside the house. In wealthier households, some armour might be put on show. Here are some carp kites that are flown today to celebrate the boys' festival. ▶

◀ A dolls festival was celebrated by girls on 3 March. Dolls which were meant to look like the Emperor and Empress of Japan, together with their family and servants, were put on display in the house. Special drinks and sweet cakes were eaten as part of this festival.

29

GLOSSARY

Abacus A wooden frame which has beads that slide up and down for counting.

Apprentice A person who is learning a craft and makes promises to stay with their employer.

Bunraku Theatre where puppets are used to tell the story.

Ceramics A type of pottery.

Confucianism The ideas of Confucius, a Chinese teacher of morals and human values.

Geisha A woman who is trained to entertain guests by singing, dance, music and witty conversation.

Inro A small container used to hold medicine or other small objects.

Kabuki Theatre based on popular stories full of exciting acting and attractive costumes.

Kimono A long, loose robe worn with a belt.

Lacquer A hard varnish placed on objects.

Noh Theatre performed on a plain stage. The performers move in a slow and elegant way.

Pilgrimage To go on a journey to a sacred place.

Porters People employed to carry packages.

Samurai The warrior class.

Shintoism Japan's traditional religion where nature is seen as sacred.

Shogun A military leader.

Shrine A place where gods are worshipped.

Silk-worms Worms which make a fine silk thread.

Tea ceremony A formal occasion when tea is served in a special way.

Tea-houses Places where refreshments and various kinds of entertainment could be bought.

Temples Buildings where Buddhist gods are worshipped.

IMPORTANT DATES

1600   The Tokugawa family begin their rule of Japan. This was to last for the next 250 years.

1603   Tokugawa Ieyasu receives the title of shogun from the emperor. Ieyasu makes Edo the new capital of Japan.

1639   The shogun forbids all contact with the outside world.

1657   The Great Fire of Meireki burns down large areas of Edo city.

1675-1725   Genroku period. This time was famous for the growth of culture and the arts.

1700   Edo is thought to have been the largest city in the world at this time.

1854   The American seaman Commodore Matthew Perry lands in Japan. This visit opens up contact between Japan and Western countries.

1855   Great Edo earthquake.

1867-8   The last shogun hands over power to the Japanese Emperor. The Emperor moves to Edo and rules Japan.

BOOKS TO READ

How They Lived – A Samurai Warrior by Anne Steel (Wayland, 1986)
This book tells you about the lives of the samurai warriors in the seventeenth century. Many details about their everyday lives are described.

Souvenirs From Japan by Magarita Winkel (Bamboo, 1991)
A collection of nineteenth-century photographs from the Schilling Collection showing life in Japan at that time.

INDEX